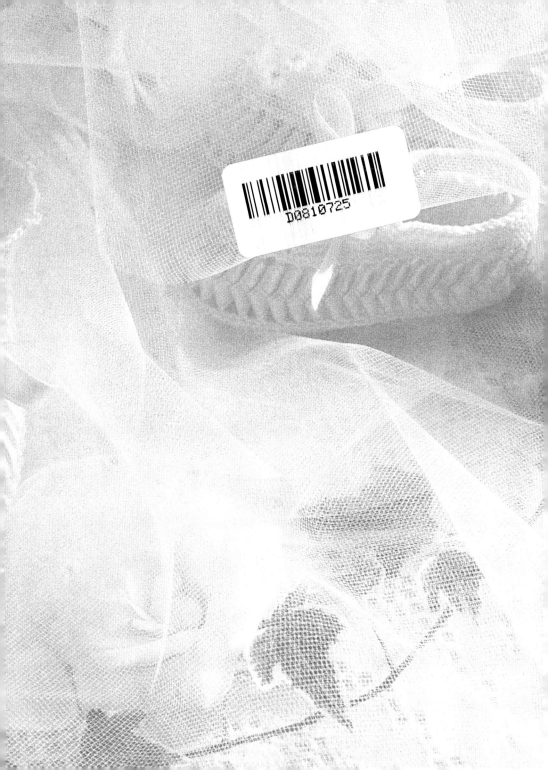

Victoria

A LOVE IS BORN

Victoria

A love is born

A NEW MOTHER'S KEEPSAKE JOURNAL

HEARST BOOKS

NEW YORK

All permissions and copyright credits appear on pages 138-143. Recognizing the importance of preserving what has been written, it is the policy of William Morrow and Company, Inc., and its imprints and affiliates to have the books it publishes printed on acid-free paper, and we exert our best efforts to that end.

Victoria a love is born
A collection of recollections from many generations of writers enhanced by quotations and illustrations from *Victoria* magazine. Published in a journal format so that readers can chronicle their own recollections.
ISBN: 0-688-04930-9

Printed in Singapore
First U.S. Edition
1 2 3 4 5 6 7 8 9 10

For Victoria -
Nancy Lindemeyer, Editor
Bryan E. McCay, Art Director
John Mack Carter, Director, Magazine Development

Edited by Linda Sunshine
Designed by Nina Ovryn
Produced by Smallwood & Stewart, Inc., New York City

NOTICE: Every effort has been made to locate the copyright owners of the material used in this book. Please let us know if an error has been made, and we will make any necessary changes in subsequent printings.

A baby is
God's opinion that
the world should
go on.

Carl Sandburg

$\mathcal{I}$NTRODUCTION

ictoria is a magazine dedicated to the celebration of family and the tradition of generations. We believe that giving birth is life's most powerful realization of a miracle. "Birth is not one act, it is a process," wrote Erich Fromm. And that ever-changing process, the flowering of life from pregnancy to childbirth, filled with the most profound human emotions, is the focus of this illustrated journal.

In *A Love Is Born*, we have gathered together the wisdom and philosophy of generations of writers who have witnessed and explored the phenomenon of bringing forth new life into the world. Mary Gordon once wrote, "No one had told her what it would be like, the way she loved her children." We hope that the words in this volume will open a window into the rich and joyous process that has begun within you. It is also our hope that by adding your own thoughts and feelings to this journal, you will be creating a keepsake journal for yourself, your children, and your children's children.

The Editors, Victoria

Life is
always
a rich and
steady time
when you
are waiting for
something
to happen or to
hatch.

E. B. White
Charlotte's Web

A Prayer for My Daughter

Once more the storm is howling,

and half hid under

this cradle-hood and coverlid

my child sleeps on.

William Butler Yeats

WHEN WE FOUND OUT ABOUT BABY

That was July. By September, she was having to
leave the waistband of her jeans unsnapped and she
wore her loosest work shirts over them. She said
she thought she could feel the baby moving now ~ a little
bubble, she said, flitting here and there in a larking sort
of way. Ian set a palm on her abdomen but it was still
too early for him to feel anything from outside.

She bought a book that showed what the baby
looked like week by week, and she and Ian studied it
together. A lima bean. A tadpole. Then finally a person
but a clumsily constructed one, like something modeled
in preschool. They were thinking of Joshua for a boy and
Rachel for a girl. Ian tried the names on his tongue
to see how they'd work in everyday life. "Oh, and I'd like
you to meet my son, Joshua Bedloe . . . " His son!

Anne Tyler
Saint Maybe

I have outgrown
my wedding dress, and it will no longer
cover one beating heart only!
O Father, let the child but be
as happy, and far better, than the mother
and I pray for no other boon. . . .
Let me strive to be all truth
and gentleness and heavenly mindedness,
to be already the guardian-angel
of my child.

Fanny Appleton Longfellow

THE EVENING STAR

O, *my beloved,* . . .
My morning and my evening star of love! . . .
Even thus,
As that fair planet in the sky above,
Dost thou retire unto thy rest at night,
And from thy darkened window fades
the light.

Henry Wadsworth Longfellow

THOUGHTS ABOUT BEING PREGNANT

As we returned toward her house, stepping carefully over the rocks, I wondered about that child moving in the mysterious inland sea of Annie Kate's body. I held her hand and realized that the blood I felt rushing through her wrist would soon be rushing through the brain of the fetus, that her body had become an aquarium and that her child was a swimmer in its lightless pool. We were three human hearts on that walk down the beach, three different views of the universe, three sets of aligned yet separate dreams.

I wondered if I had dreamed in my mother's womb. What would be the first dream in a newly created brain ~ perhaps some ancient common dream of the species, an image of fire or the first shuddering memory of stars or bison on the walls of caverns? Or do the dreams of mothers become the dreams of the half-children? Did I dream my mother's dreams? Did I learn of roses and aircraft and snow-fall because my mother's dreams had traveled her body with their images intact and electric and full of messages from the outside world?

Pat Conroy, Lords of Discipline

She named the infant "Pearl," as being of a great price, ~ purchased with all she had, ~ her mother's only treasure!. . . By its perfect shape, its vigor, and its natural dexterity in the use of all its untried limbs, the infant was worthy to have been brought forth in Eden; worthy to have been left there, to be the plaything of the angels, after the world's first parents were driven out. . . . Pearl's aspect was imbued with a spell of infinite variety; in this one child there were many children, com-prehending the full scope between the wild-flower prettiness of a peasant-baby, and the pomp, in little, of an infant princess.

> *Nathaniel Hawthorne*
> **The Scarlet Letter**

My First Trimester

In this golden morning
the pollen of abundance lifts from the
dust of years of drought:
It will be the year of our baby.
I wish for one thing: That you may
give her a soul like yours.
That you may bring her always
through forests, treasures, battles,
loves to the centre of a horizon from
which one can dominate the world.
That you may let her fly lightly
following the track of your butterfly
wing, like a golden powder
on the leaves which may guide her
through the thickets.
I love you both. P.

From Paolo to Kuki Gallman
on the impending birth of their
daughter, Sveva. Paolo died in a car
accident several months before his
daughter was born.

Kuki Gallman
I Dreamed of Africa

THE WONDER-CHILD

"Our little babe," each said, "shall be
Like unto thee" ~ "Like unto thee!"
    "Her mother's" ~ "Nay, his father's" ~ "eyes,"
    "Dear curls like thine" ~ but each replies,
"As thine, all thine, and naught of me."

What sweet solemnity to see
The little life upon thy knee,
    And whisper as so soft it lies, ~
      "Our little babe!"

For, whether it be he or she,
A David or a Dorothy,
    "As mother fair," or "father wise,"
    Both when it's "good," and when it cries,
One thing is certain, ~ it will be
    Our little babe.

Richard Le Gallienne

ALL IS VANIT

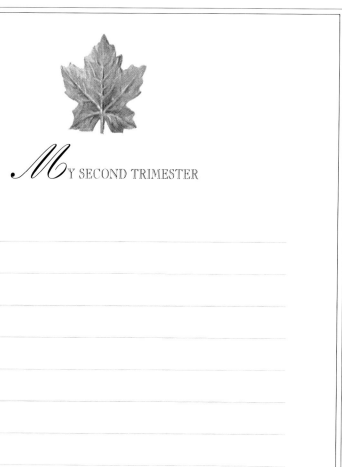

$\mathcal{M}$Y SECOND TRIMESTER

So reliant
is the intimacy
between
Nature and her
children, she
addresses them
as "comrades
in arms."

Emily Dickinson

My Third Trimester

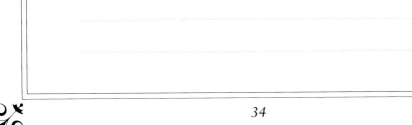

The world

has no such flower

in any land,

And no such pearl in any

gulf the sea,

As any babe on

any mother's knee.

Pelagius

*T*he actual experience of being a mother is one of
the most fulfilling I've ever had. Pregnancy was the most
continuous happiness I've known. Each time I've
experienced birth there's been an overbearing feeling of loss,
in the hospital right after the baby's birth, when
the baby would be taken into the nursery. And then the
greatest flooding of joy when the baby would be
brought back to me.

Gloria Vanderbilt
Woman to Woman

$\mathscr{B}$ABY'S BIRTH

*I*t is almost impossible for a
mother to separate the reality of her child from the
abstract idea of her child, and some women
never do this at all. . . .
Then there was this child after nine long months
and, suddenly, Duff was no longer an idea
but a fact. There was no question of loving that girl.
None at all. And, because of her circumstances
prior to having her (that is, lusting after
water and seeing in Preston someone who would take
her to that water ~ or, less dreamily and
more pragmatically, the fact of impending motherhood
when she was unprepared for it), it was as
if the pregnancy and the birth were
truly two separate things that each had the power to
open and close Sophia's world.

Whitney Otto
How to Make an American Quilt

THE PRINCESS

*H*appy he
With such a mother!
Faith in womankind
Beats with his blood.

Alfred, Lord Tennyson

When you came into the world, my last born, Minet-Chéri, I suffered for three days and two nights. When I was carrying you I was as big as a house. Three days seems a long time. . . . But I've never regretted my suffering. They do say that children like you, who have been carried so high in the womb and have taken so long to come down into the daylight, are always the children that are most loved, because they have lain so near their mother's heart and have been so unwilling to leave her."

Colette
My Mother's House and Sido

All winter Wilbur watched over Charlotte's egg sac as though he were guarding his own children. He had scooped out a special place in the manure for the sac, next to the board fence. On very cold nights he lay so that his breath would warm it. For Wilbur, nothing in life was so important as this small, round object ~ nothing else mattered. Patiently he awaited the end of winter and the coming of the little spiders. . . .

One fine sunny morning, after breakfast, Wilbur stood watching his precious sac. He wasn't thinking of anything much. As he stood there, he noticed something move. He stepped closer and stared. A tiny spider crawled from the sac. It was no bigger than a grain of sand, no bigger than the head of a pin. Its body was grey with a black stripe underneath. Its legs were grey and tan. It looked just like Charlotte.

Wilbur trembled all over when he saw it. The little

spider waved at him. Then Wilbur looked more closely. Two more little spiders crawled out and waved. They climbed round and round on the sac, exploring their new world. Then three more little spiders. Then eight. Then ten. Charlotte's children were here at last.

Wilbur's heart pounded. He began to squeal. Then he raced in circles, kicking manure into the air. Then he turned a back flip. Then he planted his front feet and came to a stop in front of Charlotte's children.

"Hello, there!" he said.

The first spider said hello, but its voice was so small Wilbur couldn't hear it.

"I am an old friend of your mother's," said Wilbur. "I'm glad to see you. Are you all right? Is everything all right?"

The little spiders waved their forelegs at him. Wilbur could see by the way they acted that they were glad to see him.

E. B. White
Charlotte's Web

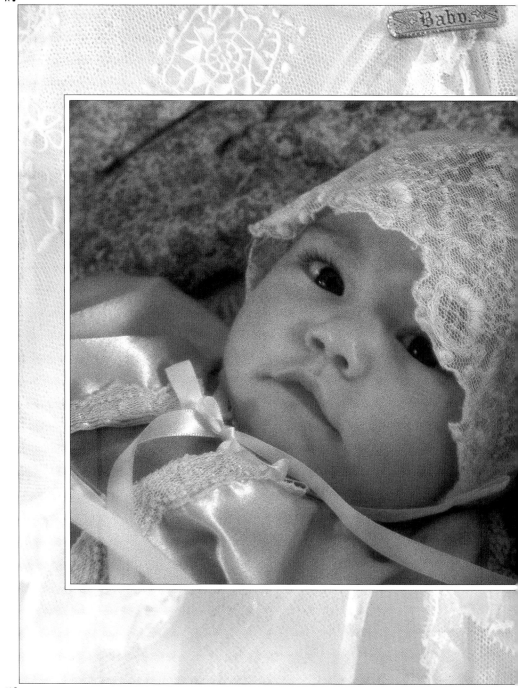

FRIDAY, [NOV 10]
DEC 31, 1819
I have not kept my Journal
all this time; but I have little to say,
except that on the morning
of Friday, November 12,
little Percy Florence was born.

TUES, DEC 2, 1834
My heart and soul is bound up in
Percy. My race is run.

JUNE 1, 1840
If I could restore health,
administer balm to the wounded
heart, and banish care from those
I love, I were in myself happy,
while I am loved and Percy continues
the blessing that he is.

Mary Shelley
Her Journal

*T*he Angel that presided
o'er my birth
Said, "Little creature, formed
of much joy and mirth,
Go love with out the help of
Anything on Earth."

William Blake

GIFTS FROM MOTHER

I begin to love this little creature, and to anticipate his birth as a fresh twist to a knot, which I do not wish to untie.

Mary Wollstonecraft

his child of hers seemed to have been made of a different material from the rest of the human race. Even before she was born, Nívea had known she was not of this world, because she had already seen her in dreams. This was why she had not been surprised when the midwife screamed as the child emerged. At birth Rosa was white and smooth, without a wrinkle, like a porcelain doll, with green hair and yellow eyes ~ the most beautiful creature to be born on earth since the days of original sin, as the midwife put it, making the sign of the cross. From her very first bath, Nana had washed her hair with camomile, which softened its color, giving it the hue of old bronze, and put her out in the sun with nothing on, to strengthen her skin, which was translucent in the most delicate parts of her chest and armpits, where the veins and secret texture of the muscles could be seen. Nana's gypsy tricks did not suffice, however, and rumors quickly spread that Nívea had borne an angel.

Isabel Allende
The House of the Spirits

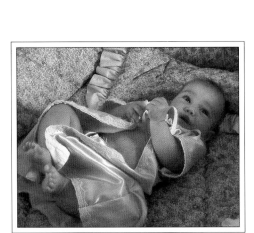

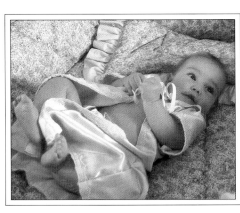

*B*egin, baby boy, to

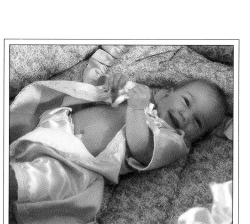
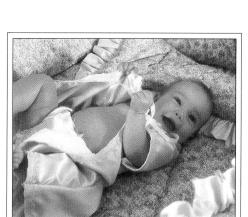

recognize your mother with a smile.

Virgil

When the first baby
laughed for the first time, the laugh
broke into a thousand pieces
and they all went skipping about and
that was the beginning of fairies.

J. M. *Barrie*
Peter Pan

 y young monkey has become, in five months, the prettiest creature that ever a mother bathed with her happy tears, washed, brushed, combed, decked out; for God knows with what an indefatigable ardor those little flowers are decked out, clothed, brushed, washed, changed, kissed! Well then, my monkey is no longer a monkey, but a *baby*, as my English nurse says, a pink and white *baby*; and, as he feels himself loved, he does not cry too much; but, in truth, I scarcely ever leave him and I endeavor to penetrate him with my soul. . . . The joy of a mother is a light which is thrown even on the future and lightens it up, but which is reflected on the past to give it the charm of souvenirs.

. . . As for myself, my dear soul, I am from moment to moment more happy. Each hour brings a new bond between a mother and her infant. . . . Ah! how many things an infant teaches its mother.

Honoré de Balzac
Memoirs of Two Young Wives

Sleep, baby, sleep,

Our cottage vale is deep:

The little lamb is on the green,

With wooly fleece so soft and clean-

Sleep, baby, sleep.

Sleep, baby, sleep,

Down where the woodbines creep;

Be always like the lamb so mild,

A kind, and sweet, and gentle child.

Sleep, baby, sleep.

Mother Goose

Life is
the first gift,
love is the
second, and
understanding
the third.

Marge Piercy

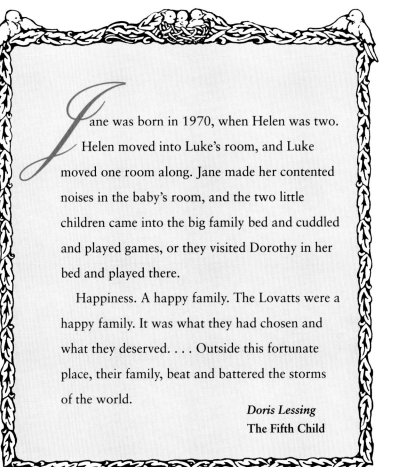

ane was born in 1970, when Helen was two. Helen moved into Luke's room, and Luke moved one room along. Jane made her contented noises in the baby's room, and the two little children came into the big family bed and cuddled and played games, or they visited Dorothy in her bed and played there.

Happiness. A happy family. The Lovatts were a happy family. It was what they had chosen and what they deserved. . . . Outside this fortunate place, their family, beat and battered the storms of the world.

Doris Lessing
The Fifth Child

TO ALFRED TENNYSON, MY GRANDSON

Golden-hair'd Ally whose name is one with mine,
Crazy with laughter and babble and earth's new wine,
Now that the flower of a year and a half is thine,
O little blossom, O mine, and mine of mine,
Glorious poet who never hast written a line,
Laugh, for the name at the head of my verse is thine,
May'st thou never be wrong'd by the name that is mine!

Alfred, Lord Tennyson

*M*Y FATHER'S LEGACY

A WEEK OF BIRTHDAYS

Monday's child is fair of face,

Tuesday's child is full of grace,

Wednesday's child is full of woe,

Thursday's child has far to go,

Friday's child is loving and giving,

Saturday's child works hard for its living

But the child that's born on the Sabbath day

Is bonny and blithe, and good and gay.

Mother Goose

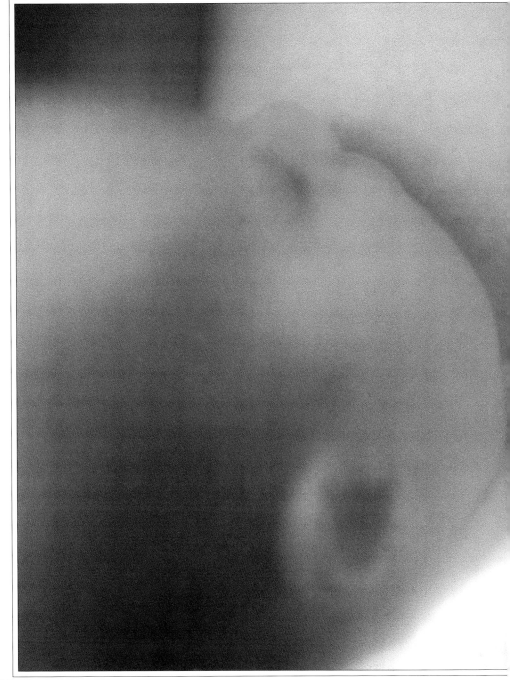

After delivery, Maman's body entered upon still another phase. When she first felt her son's groping mouth attach itself to her breast, a wave of sweet vibration thrilled deep inside and radiated to all parts of her body; it was similar to love, but it went beyond a lover's caress, it brought a great calm happiness. She had never experienced that feeling before; when her lover had kissed her breast, it had been a brief moment that was supposed to have made up for hours of doubt and mistrust; but now she knew that a mouth was attached to her breast with unending devotion, a devotion of which she could be perfectly certain.

. . . Ah, the joy of suckling! She lovingly watched the fishlike motions of the toothless mouth and she imagined that with her milk there flowed into her little son her deepest thoughts, concepts, and dreams.

Milan Kundera
Life Is Elsewhere

There is
no finer
investment
for any
community
than putting
milk into
babies.

Winston Churchill

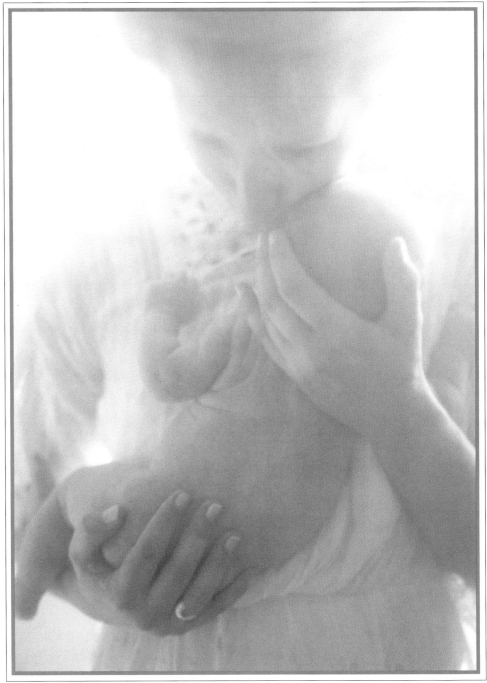

O young thing,
your mother's lovely armful!
How sweet the
fragrance of your body!

Euripides

Families, when a child is born
Want it to be intelligent.
I, through intelligence,
Having wrecked my whole life,
Only hope the baby will prove
Ignorant and stupid.
Then he will crown a tranquil life
By becoming a Cabinet Minister.

Su Tung-P'o

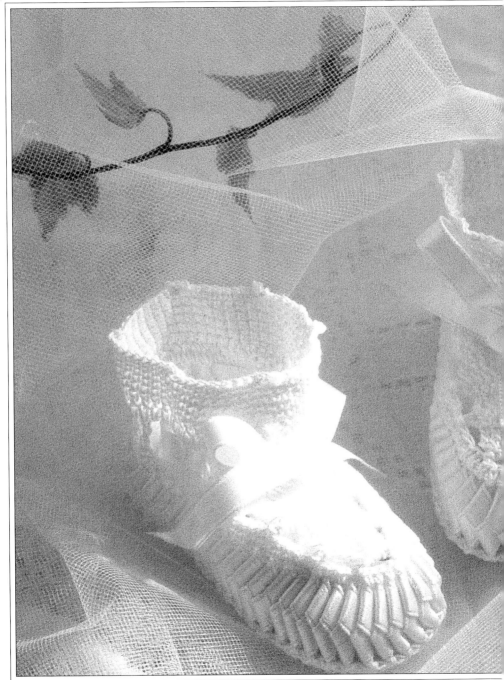

Being a mother is an
excitement, an enticement,
and a growth. It is the possibility
that haunts and delights
the young girl as she grows
to womanhood. It is part of the
fantasy, both her longing for it and
her fear of it. The months of
pregnancy highlight all the
richness of the remembered and
internalized experience about
mothering. The birth itself brings
forth the baby, until now a
fantasy, into reality. This real baby
is a constant changing, crying,
knowing being, and for me the
delight of this experience has been
one of the most important parts of
my life as a woman.

Dr. Beverly Raphael

I thank the goodness and the grace

Which on my birth have smiled,

And made me, in these Christian days,

A happy English child.

Ann and Jane Taylor
Hymns for Infant Minds

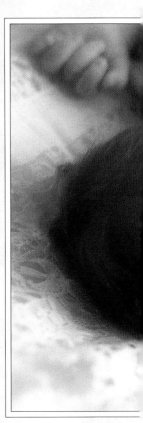

O hush thee, my babie,
thy sire was a knight.
Thy mother a lady,
both lovely and bright.

Sir Walter Scott
Lullaby of an Infant Chief

*F*rom the kitchen
she went into the hall and
from there to the nursery. She had
left the door partially open, and
now she entered the room softly. A
small, rose-shaded night light
burned in one corner, atop the ivory
chest of drawers, and the crib
stood in the opposite corner, against
the wall. Moving toward the
crib, the girl paused by it, looking
downward and smiling. A dark fuzz
of hair lay against the white
satin pillows, and below it was a
profiled roundness of cream and pink,
bounded by blue blankets. He slept.
Mr. Timothy Ryder, Jr., slept.
"Hello, Tim," whispered
the girl, leaning over the rail of the
crib. "Hello, Timmy. My baby,
my baby, my baby."

Richard Sherman
Barrow Street

*H*omer and Candy loved how they fit together in the bed again and how Angel could fit between them when Candy was nursing him, and how Candy's milk would sometimes wake them both up before Angel's crying would. They agreed: they had never been happier. So what if the sky, when it was almost May, was still the slate color of February, and still streaked with sleet? So what if the secret they kept at St. Cloud's could not be kept forever ~ and was already a secret that half of Heart's Haven and Heart's Rock had the sense to figure out for themselves? People from Maine don't crowd you; they let you come to your senses in your own, good time.

John Irving
Cider House Rules

*F*amily love is this

dynastic awareness of time, this shared

belonging to a chain of generations . . .

we collaborate together to root

each other in a dimension of time longer

than our own lives.

Michael Ignatieff
Lodged in the Heart and Memory

OUR FAMILY TREE

_____
Great-Grandmother

_____
Great-Grandmother

_____
Great-Grandfather

_____
Great-Grandfather

_____
Great-Grandmother

_____
Great-Grandmother

_____
Great-Grandfather

_____
Great-Grandfather

_____
Grandmother   Grandfather

_____
Grandmother   Grandfather

_____
Mother

_____
Father

_____
Baby's Name

*A*nd she was proud
of me, prouder still of having had me when
she did. Photos show and I remember
her holding me up showing me off like a
Campbell's commercial might a fine
new can of soup, me all dolled up in lace
and what looked like doilies.
The Ivory baby. She'd said I looked like
the Ivory flakes baby.

Linnea Johnson

ou
were such a wanted baby.
I would
rub my belly in awe of
your growing.
Sit motionless waiting
for your kicks
and stretches. Think of you,
wonder about you,
wait for you ~ totally caught in
the miracle of your
coming to life.
First Child, child of hope,
child of commitment.

Julie Owen Edwards

ℬooks for Baby

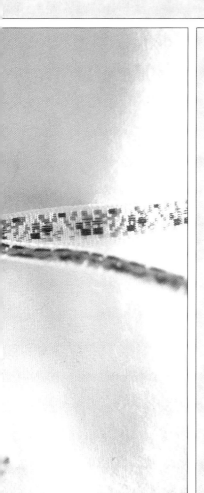

 was their
plaything and their idol, and
something better ~ their child, the
innocent and helpless creature
bestowed on them by heaven, whom
to bring up to good, and whose future
lot it was in their hands to direct to
happiness or misery, according as
they fulfilled their duties
towards me. With this deep
consciousness of what they owed
towards the being to which
they had given life, added to the active
spirit of tenderness that animated
both, it may be imagined that
while during every hour of my infant
life I received a lesson of
patience, of charity, and of self-
control, I was so guided by a silken
cord that all seemed but one train
of enjoyment to me.
Mary Wollstonecraft Shelley

FAMILY LEGENDS

FROST AT MIDNIGHT

*D*ear Babe, that sleepest cradled by my side,

Whose gentle breathings, heard in this deep calm,

Fill up the interspersed vacancies

And momentary pauses of the thought!

My babe so beautiful! it thrills my heart

With tender gladness, thus to look at thee,

And think that thou shalt learn far other lore

And in far other scenes!

Samuel Taylor Coleridge

GIFTS FOR BABY

She sat back for a moment. I could see only her head and shoulders over the scarred formica between us. She was blond, paler blond than I. Even though she'd turned three a few months before, her hair was still really nothing but wisps clinging to the shape of her skull. But her body was sturdy, and she had delicate, completely regular features. Except for her nose, which was unusually long ~ strong, I liked to call it ~ for a child her age. We had called her the Schnozz when she was an infant, in order to mask our fears that she'd grow up to be ugly. Now I couldn't tell anymore if she was ugly or not. I never tired of looking at her. Sometimes she'd find it annoying, as though I were taking something from her by loving her so greedily with my eyes. 'Don't *look* at me, Mommy,' she'd say, and cover her eyes with her hands as though then I couldn't see her anymore.

Sue Miller
The Good Mother

And he who gives a child a treat

Makes joy-bells ring in Heaven's street,

And he who gives a child a home

Builds palaces in Kingdom come.

John Masefield
Pompeii the Great

HOW YOU GOT YOUR NAME

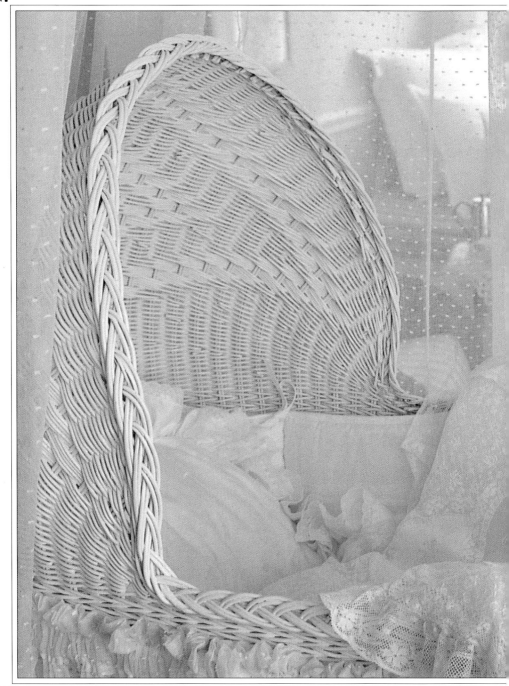

THE CRADLE

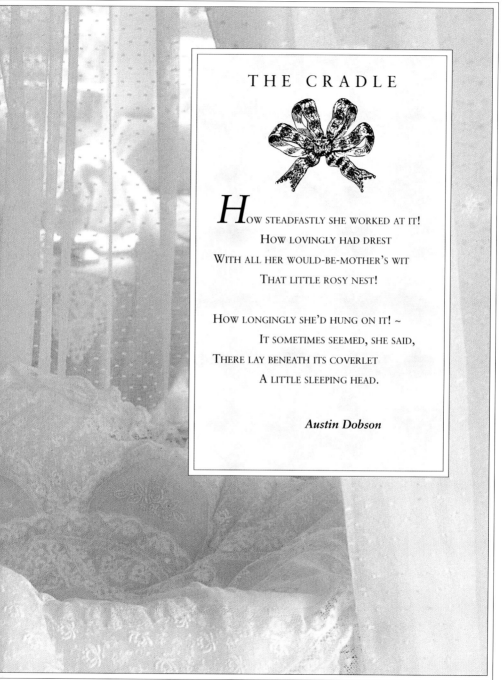

How steadfastly she worked at it!
How lovingly had drest
With all her would-be-mother's wit
That little rosy nest!

How longingly she'd hung on it! ~
It sometimes seemed, she said,
There lay beneath its coverlet
A little sleeping head.

Austin Dobson

"*I* was in you," she said suddenly, poking at her mother's stomach.

"Who told you that?" Emma asked.

"Teddy," Melanie said.

"I could have guessed. Teddy's a blabbermouth."

"Un-uh, you're a blabbermouth," Melanie said. "Tell me the truth."

Emma laughed. "What truth?"

"I was in you," Melanie said, nodding her head affirmatively. She was very curious.

"Yes, you were, now that you bring it up," Emma said. "So what?"

Melanie felt triumphant. She had confirmed a secret.

"So what, so what, so what," she said, and fell on her mother. "Let's sing some songs."

Larry McMurtry
Terms of Endearment

'Do you know who made you?'
'Nobody, as I knows of,' said the child, with a
short laugh . . . 'I 'spect I grow'd.'

Harriet Beecher Stowe
Uncle Tom's Cabin

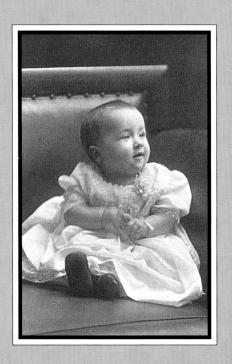

Love them,
feed them,
discipline them
and let them
go free.
You may have a
life-long good
relationship.

Mary G. L. Davis

LITTLE BIRDIE

*W*hat does little birdie say,
In her nest, at peep of day?
   "Let me fly," says little birdie,
   "Mother, let me fly away." ~
"Birdie, rest a little longer,
Till the little wings are stronger."
So she rests a little longer,
   Then she flies away.

What does the little baby say,
In her bed, at peep of day?
   Baby says, like a little birdie,
   "Let me rise and fly away." ~
"Baby, sleep a little longer.
Till the little limbs are stronger.
If she sleeps a little longer,
   Baby, too, shall fly away."

Alfred, Lord Tennyson

WHERE DID YOU COME FROM, BABY DEAR?
OUT OF THE EVERYWHERE INTO THE HERE.

WHERE DID YOU GET THOSE EYES SO BLUE?
OUT OF THE SKY AS I CAME THROUGH.

WHAT MAKES THE LIGHT IN THEM SPARKLE AND SPIN?
SOME OF THE STARRY SPIKES LEFT IN.

WHERE DID YOU GET THAT LITTLE TEAR?
I FOUND IT WAITING WHEN I GOT HERE.

WHAT MAKES YOUR FOREHEAD SO SMOOTH AND HIGH?
A SOFT HAND STROK'D IT AS I WENT BY.

WHAT MAKES YOUR CHEEK LIKE A WARM WHITE ROSE?
I SAW SOMETHING BETTER THAN ANY ONE KNOWS.

WHENCE THAT THREE-CORNER'D SMILE OF BLISS?
THREE ANGELS GAVE ME AT ONCE A KISS.

WHERE DID YOU GET THIS PEARLY EAR?
GOD SPOKE, AND IT CAME OUT TO HEAR.

WHERE DID YOU GET THOSE ARMS AND HANDS?
LOVE MADE ITSELF INTO BONDS AND BANDS.

FEET, WHENCE DID YOU COME, YOU DARLING THINGS?
FROM THE SAME BOX AS THE CHERUBS' WINGS.

HOW DID THEY ALL JUST COME TO BE YOU?
GOD THOUGHT ABOUT ME, AND SO I GREW.

BUT HOW DID YOU COME TO US, YOU DEAR?
GOD THOUGHT ABOUT YOU, AND SO I AM HERE.

George Macdonald
Baby

W A N T E D :

FEMALE FOR MOTHER,
NO EXPERIENCE NECESSARY, NO
PRE-TRAINING GIVEN. HOURS: 24 HOUR
SHIFT FOR LIFE OF CHILD. SALARY:
MEAGER, GOVERNMENT SUBSIDIZED,
$3.79 PER WEEK. HOLIDAY AND SICK
LEAVE NEGOTIABLE, BUT NOT
ENCOURAGED. THOROUGH GROUNDING
AN ADVANTAGE IN:
NURSING
CATERING
PHILOSOPHY
PSYCHIATRY
SEX
RELIGION
CARPENTRY
DRESSMAKING
MARKETING & FINANCE
MEDIA APPRECIATION
TAXI DRIVING
ARTS
SCIENCE
AND SPORT
END RESULT HIGHLY UNPREDICTABLE,
PRODUCT NON-EXCHANGEABLE AND
NON-RETURNABLE. COULD BE FUN
AND REWARDING.

Jan Power
Positions Vacant, Women & Girls

You must resist the tendency to think ahead; wishing for peace is *not* the same thing as wanting things to change forever, and when all is said and done (a state only songwriters believe in), the child will never really be gone, even though he grows up. You will find that although the child may be remembered in association with one or two prized toys, more likely the child will be remembered alone, standing with his legs parted, his arms dangling at his sides, pants fallen a bit so that only the toes of the sneakers are visible. He will be standing the way he stood in the snapshot, with an expanse of field ~ or maybe the beach ~ around him. A little thing, but you will remember that distinctly without having a photograph in front of you. That will be the way, in fact, the child will stay: a visual image ~ one that, even at the time, you squinted to look harder at, whether or not a camera was raised to your eye.

When you are thirty, the child is two. At forty, you realize that the child in the house, the child you live with, is still, when you close your eyes, or the moment he has walked from the room, two years old. When you are sixty, and the child is gone, the child will also be two, but then you will be more certain. Seeing pictures of your child at different ages, you will not hesitate for a moment. You will point to the two-year-old, not the ten-year-old or the twenty-year-old. He will always be that high. With a nick above the eyebrow. Those eyes, at that point a bit too large for his face, so that, in remembering the eyes, you are sure that your

child possessed startling intensity. He might be wearing some article of clothing purchased for a special occasion, but unless the picture of the shirt with the anchor and the sheep-shank knot is right in front of you, you will not think much about that. He will be in typical little-boy clothes, smiling or looking straight at the camera with a tolerant expression that may show a hint of fatigue: Another picture? Why do you want it? What can it mean to you? He will be there with you without special costumes or toys as the years go by: the child alone, more and more a fact. Your life before the child seems too long ago to think of. What happened with the child, something of a blur. There were late-night walks in the summer heat, weren't there? Didn't the child once assume that you could give him

pointers about how to fly? Didn't he think he was recreating the rumbling of Vesuvius with the plastic straw in the glass of chocolate milk? You go on ~ and the child goes on ~ but you change, as the child sees you. You do, but he does not. He stays the same, no matter how many marriages, mortgages, dogs, and children he may surround himself with ~ he does not change, so he is not vulnerable. It becomes difficult to remember that he ever was. That the dog snapped at him, and he was afraid. That the cut got infected. That night after night, the same blue-bodied demon flicked its tail in his dreams. Sticky fingers. Wet sheets. Wet kisses. A flood of tears. As you remember him, the child is always two.

Ann Beattie
Picturing Will

Her court was pure; her life serene;
God gave her peace; her land reposed;
A thousand claims to reverence closed
In her as Mother, Wife, and Queen.

Alfred, Lord Tennyson
To the Queen

*S*ome things go to sleep in such a funny way.
Little birds stand on one leg and tuck their head away.

Chickens do the same standing on their perch;
Little mice lie soft and still as if they were in a church;

Kittens curl up close in such a funny ball,
Horses hang their sleepy heads and stand still in a stall;

Sometimes dogs stretch out, or curl up in a heap;
Cows lie down upon their sides when they would go to sleep.

But little babies dear are snugly tucked in beds,
Warm with blankets, all so soft, and pillows for their heads.

Bird and beast and babe ~ I wonder which of all
Dream the dearest dreams that down from dreamland fall!

Alfred, Lord Tennyson

H ave you ever seen eyes so blue?' The doctor was holding out the baby for me to see. 'A beautiful baby girl. Well done.'

I had been waiting for this moment during the long months, listening to the baby kicking in my enlarged belly, resting in the afternoons, embroidering a cushion in needlepoint with the words: FOR PAOLO'S BABY. Eating the right food, going through exercises, check-ups, scans: nothing should go wrong for the birth of Paolo's child. Always I listened to the music of Boccherini, which had a soothing effect on me.

In view of the problems I had gone through, and my age, the doctor had suggested that, if the baby was late, they would induce it. I had chosen a prospective date, which sounded like a good omen: 18.8.80.

On the chosen date, the baby was born naturally. It was 4.35 a.m. She weighed eight pounds and was fifty-one centimetres long.

I had arrived at Nairobi Hospital feeling well, with a great sense of expectation, an unbearable curiosity. The nurse kept coming back to check, a puzzled look on her face. I was in labour. From the headphones around my head, from

the ones around my belly the music flew, taking away the pain, submerging us both in waves of pure harmony. The music Paolo had loved and chosen for his funeral was going to be the music of this re-birth. The baby was born with the music as the only medicine. And she was not crying.

It is a unique moment, that first meeting of a mother and her new-born baby, the first glance at the mysterious creature that for months has been carried and nursed in the secret of the womb, and now has become a different, forever independent human being, with features inherited from generations of ancestors.

I held out my hands. Perfect head, tanned skin, dark golden fuzz of hair, and, extraordinary for a new-born baby, open, direct, intense and knowing blue eyes.

'A sign, just give me a sign.'

Slowly, almost deliberately, while the deep-blue eyes never left mine, the index finger of the left hand curled up tightly, and she grabbed my hand with the other fingers. Weakness, relief, joy at the pit of my stomach.

'Welcome back,' I whispered, before I finally slept.

Kuki Gallman
I Dreamed of Africa

Cover: Photograph by Elyse Lewin.

7: Photograph by Starr Ockenga.

8-9: Photograph by Toshi Otsuki. Excerpt from *Charlotte's Web* by E. B. White. Copyright © 1952 by Harper and Row. Reprinted with permission of HarperCollins Publishers.

10-11: Photograph by Toshi Otsuki. Excerpt from "A Prayer for My Daughter," *Easter 1916* by William Butler Yeats.

12: Background photograph by Toshi Otsuki. Inset photograph by Monica Roberts.

13: Photograph by Monica Roberts.

14: Photograph by Toshi Otsuki.

15: Photograph by Wendi Schneider. Excerpt from *Saint Maybe* by Anne Tyler. Copyright © 1991 by Anne Tyler. Reprinted with permission of Random House, Inc.

16: Photograph by Tina Mucci.

Excerpt from Fanny Appleton Longfellow's diary dated February 1844, on the birth of her first child.

17: Background photograph by Toshi Otsuki. Inset photograph by Monica Roberts. Henry Wadsworth Longfellow's poem written to his wife, Fanny, on the birth of their second child.

18: Photograph by Luciana Pampalone.

20-21: Photograph by Monica Roberts. Excerpt from *The Lords of Discipline* by Pat Conroy. Copyright © 1980 by Pat Conroy. Reprinted with permission of Houghton Mifflin Co. All rights reserved.

22: Background photograph by Toshi Otsuki. Inset photograph by Monica Roberts.

23: Excerpt from *The Scarlet Letter* by Nathaniel Hawthorne, 1850.

24: Photograph by Monica Roberts.

26-27: Background photograph by

Toshi Otsuki. Inset photograph by Michael Skott. Excerpt from *I Dreamed of Africa* by Kuki Gallman. Copyright © 1991 by Kuki Gallman. Reprinted with permission of Viking Penguin, a division of Penguin Books USA, Inc.

28:      From "The Wonder-Child," *Volumes in Folio* by Richard Le Gallienne, 1889.

29:      Photograph by Michael Skott.

30:      Photographs by Monica Roberts.

32-33:   Photograph by Toshi Otsuki. Exerpt from a letter to Mrs. James S. Cooper by Emily Dickinson, c. 1880.

35:      Photograph by Monica Roberts.

36-37:   Photograph by Toshi Otsuki. Excerpt from the writings of Pelagius, an ancient Greek philospher.

38:      Excerpt from *Woman to Woman* by Gloria Vanderbilt. Copyright © 1979 by Gloria Vanderbilt. Reprinted with permission of Doubleday, a division of Bantam, Doubleday, Dell Publishing Group, Inc.

40:      Photograph by Monica Roberts.

41:      Excerpt from *How to Make an American Quilt* by Whitney Otto. Copyright © 1991 by Whitney Otto. Reprinted with permission of Random House, Inc.

42:      Photograph by Toshi Otsuki.

43:      Excerpt from "The Princess" by Alfred, Lord Tennyson, 1847.

44-45:   Photograph by Toshi Otsuki. Excerpt from *My Mother's House and Sido* by Colette. Copyright © 1953 by Farrar, Straus & Young. Reprinted with per-mission of Farrar, Straus & Giroux, Inc.

46-47:   Photograph by Toshi Otsuki. Excerpt from *Charlotte's Web* by E. B. White. Copyright © 1952 by Harper and Row. Reprinted with permission of HarperCollins Publishers.

48-49:   Background photograph by

Monica Roberts. Inset photograph by Elyse Lewin. Excerpts from Mary Shelley's journal, about her son, Percy.

50-51:   Photograph by Toshi Otsuki. Excerpt from "The Angel That Presided," *Notebook* by William Blake, 1807–1809.

52:     Photograph by Toshi Otsuki.

53:     Photograph courtesy of Nina Ovryn Design.

54-55:   Photograph by Toshi Otsuki. Excerpt from a letter by Mary Wollstonecraft to her husband William Godwin, June 6, 1797, awaiting the birth of her daughter, Mary Godwin.

56:     Photograph courtesy of Nina Ovryn Design.

57:     Excerpt from *The House of the Spirits* by Isabel Allende, translated from the Spanish by Magda Bogin. Copyright © 1985 by Isabel Allende. Reprinted with permission of Random House, Inc.

58-59:   Photographs by Elyse Lewin.

60-61:   Photograph by Toshi Otsuki. Excerpt from *Peter Pan* by J. M. Barrie, 1904.

62:     Photograph by Monica Roberts.

63:     Exerpt from *Memoirs of Two Young Wives* by Honoré de Balzac. Published by George Barrie and Son, 1896.

64-65:   Photograph by Monica Roberts.

66:     Photograph by Tina Mucci.

67:     Excerpt from *Gone to Soldiers* by Marge Piercy. Copyright © 1988 by Fawcett Books. Reprinted with permission of Fawcett Books.

68:     Excerpt from *The Fifth Child* by Doris Lessing. Copyright © 1988 by Alfred A. Knopf, Inc. Reprinted with permission of Random House, Inc.

69:     Photograph by Elyse Lewin.

70:     Photograph by Monica Roberts. Excerpt from "To Alfred Tennyson, My Grandson" by Alfred, Lord Tennyson, on the birth of his grandson, Ally.

72-73: Photograph by Monica Roberts.

74-75: Photograph by Monica Roberts. Excerpt from *Life Is Elsewhere* by Milan Kundera. Copyright © 1986 by Penguin Books. Reprinted with permission of Penguin Books USA, Inc.

76: Photograph by Michael Skott.

77: Excerpt from a speech by Winston Churchill, March 21, 1943.

78: Photograph by Monica Roberts.

79: From "The Mother" by Erik Lindorm. Copyright © 1963 by Sveriges Radio.

80-81: Photograph by Tina Mucci. Excerpt from a poem by Su Tung-P'o on the birth of his son, late eleventh century.

82-83: Background photograph by Michael Skott. Inset photograph by

Monica Roberts. Excerpt from *Mothers* by Dr. Beverly Raphael. Copyright © 1975 by Simon & Schuster. Reprinted with permission of The Watermark Press.

84: Photograph by Luciana Pampalone.

85: Photograph courtesy of Nina Ovryn Design. From "Hymns for Infant Minds," *A Child's Hymn of Praise* by Ann and Jane Taylor, early eighteenth century.

86-87: Photograph by Monica Roberts. Excerpt from "Lullaby of an Infant Chief" by Sir Walter Scott.

88: Photograph by Toshi Otsuki.

89: Excerpt from *Barrow Street* by Richard Sherman. Copyright © 1948 by Hearst Magazines, Inc. Copyright renewed © 1976 by N. Holmes Clare. Reprinted with permission of Harold Ober Associates.

90-91: Photograph by William P. Steele. Excerpt from *Cider House Rules* by John Irving. Copyright © 1985 by Garp Enterprises, Ltd. Reprinted with permission of Sterling Lord Literistic.

92-93:   Photograph by Elyse Lewin.
Excerpt from *Lodged in the Heart and
Memory* by Michael Ignatieff.

94:    Photograph by Starr Ockenga.

96:    Background photograph by
William P. Steele. Inset photograph by
Philippe Houze.

97:    Excerpt from "Uterus," *My
Mother's Daughter, Stories by Women*
by Linnea Johnson. Copyright © 1991 by
Linnea Johnson. Reprinted with permission of Linnea Johnson.

98-99:   Photograph by Toshi Otsuki.
Excerpt from "Motheroath" by Julie
Olsen Edwards. Reprinted with permission of *Women's Studies Quarterly,* vol.
12 no. 2.

100:    Photograph by Elyse Lewin.

101:    Photograph by Starr Ockenga.

102-103: Photograph by Toshi Otsuki.

Excerpt from *Frankenstein* by Mary
Wollstonecraft Shelley, 1818.

104:    Photograph by Starr Ockenga.

106:    Photograph by Elyse Lewin.

107:    From "Frost at Midnight" by
Samuel Taylor Coleridge, 1798.

108:    Photograph by Michael Skott.

110 :   Excerpt from *The Good Mother*
by Sue Miller. Copyright © 1986 Sue
Miller. Reprinted with permission of
HarperCollins Publishers.

111:    Photograph by Toshi Otsuki.

112:    Photograph by William P. Steele.

113:    Photograph by Toshi Otsuki.
Excerpt from "The Tragedy of Pompeii the
Great" by John Masefield, 1910.

114:    Photograph by Starr Ockenga.

116-117: Photograph by William P. Steele.
Excerpt from "The Cradle" by Austin

Dobson, late eighteenth century.

118:     Photograph by Toshi Otsuki.

119:     Excerpt from *Terms of Endearment* by Larry McMurtry. Copyright © 1975, 1989 by Larry McMurtry. Reprinted with permission of Simon & Schuster, Inc.

120:     Photograph by Elyse Lewin.

121:     Excerpt from *Uncle Tom's Cabin* by Harriet Beecher Stowe, 1852.

124:     Excerpt from "Little Birdie" by Alfred, Lord Tennyson.

125:     Photograph by Tina Mucci.

126-127: Background photograph by Michael Skott. Inset photograph by Elyse Lewin. Excerpt from "Baby" by George Macdonald, late eighteenth century.

129:     Excerpt from "Positions Vacant, Women & Girls," *Mothers* by Jan Power. Copyright © 1988 by Simon & Schuster. Reprinted with permission of

The Watermark Press.

131:     Excerpt from *Picturing Will* by Ann Beattie. Copyright © 1989 by Irony & Pity, Inc. Reprinted with permission of Random House, Inc.

133:     Excerpt from "To the Queen" by Alfred, Lord Tennyson, 1851.

137:     Excerpt from *I Dreamed of Africa* by Kuki Gallman. Copyright © 1991 by Kuki Gallman. Reprinted with permission of Viking Penguin, a division of Penguin Books USA, Inc.

Victoria

$\mathcal{B}$ABY'S $\mathcal{N}$AME _____

$\mathcal{B}$IRTH $\mathcal{D}$ATE _____